My Popsi who Lives in the Rainbows

This little girl is very lucky indeed,
because she has a ...

HUUGGGEEE family!

She has a mum, a dad, some aunts, uncles and even some cousins
She also has lots of grandparents. SIX to be exact!

There's Nanny, Pops, Grandad and Grandma, who are Daddy's parents.
Then there's Mimi and Popsi, Mummy's parents.

This little girl spends lots of time with Daddy's parents and Mimi.
But, she never ever gets to see Popsi.

This is because Popsi lives in the rainbows !

One day when the girl was at school, she told her teachers all about the man who lives in the rainbows...

The man that she calls POPS!!!!

When mummy came to pick the girl up from school, the little girl's teacher told mummy all about a wish that the girl had made.

She wished that she could find a magic phone so that her and Mummy could talk to her Popsi who lives in the rainbows.

Hearing the wish made Mummy's heart smile!

On their walk home Mummy told the girl that though it is a nice wish, it cannot come true.

Shaking her head, with a pout on her lip the girl asked ...

"Will you ever see Popsi again?"

"Will I ever meet him?"

Cradling the girl's face and touching nose to nose

Mummy said "he's always here, watching from the rainbows.

Every time the rain breaks and the sun shines into a room,

that's Popsi saying he's here and he's watching over you...

... one day when you and I have lived our lives,

and we are old and grey...

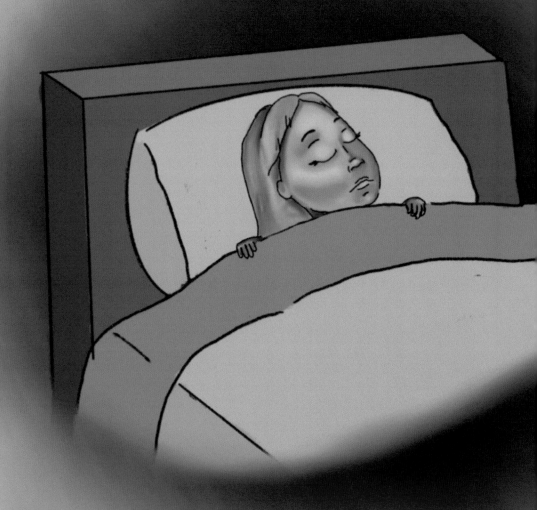

and see all the colours that are in the sky...

... because Popsi will be

standing there...

... Ready to embrace ".

The
END

For my dad (who is in
the rainbows), thank
you for introducing me
to the world of art. We
miss you.
For my daughter, thank
you for inspiring me.
Everything I do is for
you.

Printed in Great Britain
by Amazon